dream jobs ™

I want to be in
MUSICALS

PowerKiDS
press

Mary R. Dunn

Dedicated to Mary Beth

Published in 2009 by The Rosen Publishing Group, Inc.
29 East 21st Street, New York, NY 10010

First Edition

Editor: Amelie von Zumbusch
Book Design: Ginny Chu
Layout Design: Julio Gil
Photo Researcher: Jessica Gerweck

Photo Credits: Cover, pp. 4, 6, 10, 14, 18 © Getty Images; p. 8 © Serge Thomann/Getty Images; pp. 12, 16, 20 © AFP/Getty Images.

Library of Congress Cataloging-in-Publication Data

Dunn, Mary R.
  I want to be in musicals / Mary R. Dunn. — 1st ed.
     p. cm. — (Dream jobs)
  Includes index.
  ISBN 978-1-4042-4470-2 (library binding)
  1. Musicals—New York (State)—New York—Juvenile literature. I. Title.
  ML1711.8.N3D86 2009
  792.6—dc22
                                                        2007051815

Manufactured in the United States of America

Contents

The musical *Billy Elliot* is about a British boy who learns a form of dance called ballet.

Sing! Dance! Act!

When you hear a song you know, do you move to the music and sing along? Can you picture yourself on **stage**, singing and acting the part of a character? If so, maybe being in musicals is for you!

Many young **performers** enjoy taking part in musicals. A musical is a kind of play that tells a story through acting, singing, and dancing. Actors perform onstage in front of a live **audience**. Musicals are sometimes called American musicals. This is because modern musicals arose in the United States in the 1900s.

The musical *Joseph and the Amazing Technicolor Dreamcoat* is based on a story from the Bible.

Broadway Musicals

Musicals are also called Broadway musicals because many are performed in **theaters** on a street named Broadway in New York City. Broadway musicals tell many kinds of stories. The musical *Wicked* reworks *The Wizard of Oz*, a well-known movie. *Wicked* is about two witches who are characters in *The Wizard of Oz*.

The musical *Hairspray* is about a girl who wants to dance on TV. As several stage musicals are, *Hairspray* is also a movie. Other stage musicals that are also movies are *Grease*, *The Lion King*, and *The Little Mermaid*.

Along with a chandelier, the props for *The Phantom of the Opera* include standing light holders and a boat.

Broadway, Here I Come!

Boys and girls who like to act, sing, and dance generally begin in amateur musicals. These are musicals people put on for fun, not as a job. Kids in amateur musicals can gain skills and see if they really like being onstage.

Kids who want to become **professionals** often take acting classes. Students in these classes learn to follow stage directions and use props. Props are objects actors carry or use as part of a scene. In the musical *The Phantom of the Opera*, one prop is a chandelier, or hanging light holder, that falls on the stage.

Les Misérables, a musical set in France in the 1800s, ends with many characters on stage singing the song "Do You Hear the People Sing?"

Telling Stories Through Song

When you hear the words "hard-knock life," you might think of a song from the musical *Annie*. *Annie* is about a poor **orphan**. The musical has a song called "It's the Hard-Knock Life" about the hard lives orphans lead. Musicals use songs to tell a story and to show what characters are thinking.

You must sing well to perform in musicals. To become a professional, you should take singing classes to learn voice skills. Teachers point out what singers do well and what they need to practice. Learning voice skills helps actors with speaking parts, too.

This actor is dancing in *The Boy from Oz*, a musical about the life of a songwriter, named Peter Allen.

Step in Time

Just as singing classes help actors' voices, dancing lessons help actors move **gracefully** on stage. Knowing different kinds of dancing, like tap and **jazz**, gives actors a better chance of getting a part in a musical.

Sometimes, dancers perform solo, or alone on the stage. At other times, a group of actors dance together. In one fun scene in the musical *Mary Poppins*, a chimney sweep, or cleaner, called Bert, and his crew dance and jump across the rooftops of London. They dance quickly to a song called "Step in Time."

Susan Stroman directed the musical *The Producers*. Here, she is standing next to Matthew Broderick, one of the stars of that musical.

You're in the Spotlight!

Actors count on their dancing, singing, and acting skills when it comes time to audition. An audition is a test of how well a person can perform onstage.

At auditions, actors may be asked to dance and to sing a song or two. Actors also often recite, or say, a part they have learned. **Directors** watch auditions and then pick which people they want to cast, or put in the musical of which they are in charge. Directors also decide which actors are best suited to play each role, or character.

These dancers are practicing a dance from *West Side Story*, a musical about gangs in New York City.

The Hard Work Begins

You have been chosen for a part! Great! Now the director sets times for rehearsal, or practice, and the hard work begins.

There are different kinds of rehearsals. At the first rehearsal, actors might read through the whole **script**. After they learn their lines, the actors practice together, scene by scene. Cast members in dance numbers practice their dance moves. When the director thinks the cast is ready, they run through the whole performance without stopping. The last rehearsal is the dress rehearsal. The actors put on their **costumes** and use their props onstage in a dress rehearsal.

These cast members from the musical *Hairspray* are having a great time performing for the audience.

In the Glow of the Footlights

At last, it is opening night! The actors perform for their first big audience. They arrive at the theater early, do warm-ups, and check their props. The actors put on their makeup and costumes to get into character. The director generally gives a last-minute pep talk.

About 2 minutes before the play starts, the **stage manager** says, "Places, please!" A group of musicians called the orchestra starts to play. It's **curtain** time! In the glow of the footlights, actors sing and dance the parts they have rehearsed for so long.

Hugh Jackman won an honor called the Tony Award for playing Peter Allen, the main character in *The Boy from Oz*.

Broadway Stars

Great performers in musicals can become big stars. One such star is Hugh Jackman. Growing up in Sydney, Australia, Jackman played in musicals. He studied acting and was cast as Gaston in the musical *Beauty and the Beast*. In the United States, he appeared in the musical *The Boy from Oz* and in movies, such as *Happy Feet* and *X-Men*.

Bernadette Peters is a well-known Broadway actress from New York City. She started taking tap-dancing lessons when she was only three years old! Peters has played many roles, such as the pushy mother Mama Rose in the musical *Gypsy*.

You Can Be Famous!

You can play a part in musicals, too! Begin by watching musicals at the movies or on TV. Go to live musicals at theaters, too. You can even take part in plays at school and in your community. Sign up for dance lessons and learn many different steps. Taking voice lessons will prepare you for both singing and speaking parts.

Above all, audition for parts in plays. Auditioning will help you learn what you do best and what skills you still need to practice. Break a leg! In stage talk, that means "good luck!"

Glossary

audience (AH-dee-ints) A group of people who watch or listen to something.

costumes (kos-TOOMZ) Clothes that make a person look like someone or something else.

curtain (KUR-tun) A cloth that covers a window or a stage.

directors (dih-REK-terz) People who tell movie or play actors what to do.

gracefully (GRAYS-fuh-lee) Smoothly or beautifully.

jazz (JAZ) A form of dance with an easy, smooth style.

orphan (OR-fun) A child or an animal who no longer has a mother and father.

performers (per-FORM-erz) People who do something for other people to watch.

professionals (pruh-FESH-nulz) People who are paid for what they do.

script (SKRIPT) The written words of a play, movie, TV, or radio show.

stage (STAYJ) A place where people put on shows.

stage manager (STAYJ MA-nih-jer) The person who makes sure a play's script, props, actors, and timing are in order.

theaters (THEE-uh-turz) Buildings where performances are held.

Index

Web Sites

Due to the changing nature of Internet links, PowerKids Press has developed an online list of Web sites related to the subject of this book. This site is updated regularly. Please use this link to access the list: www.powerkidslinks.com/djobs/musical/